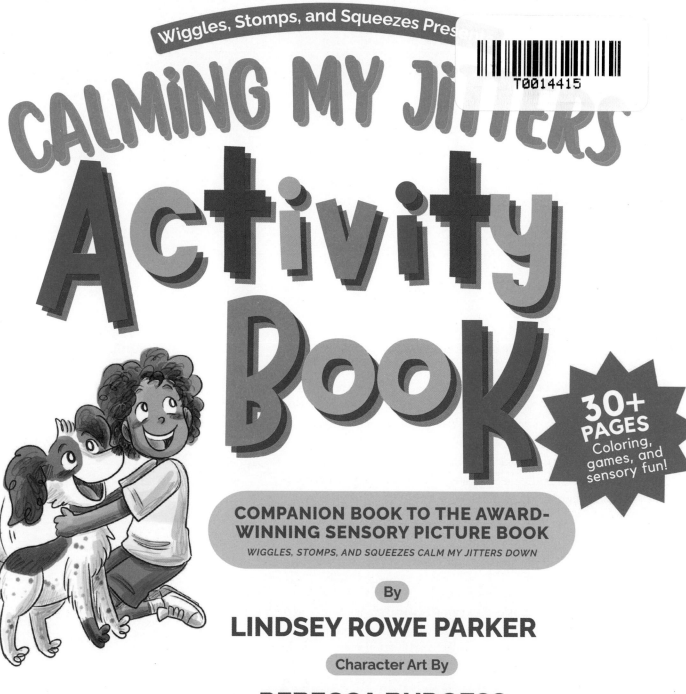

Wiggles, Stomps, and Squeezes Presents

CALMING MY JITTERS Activity Book

30+ PAGES Coloring, games, and sensory fun!

COMPANION BOOK TO THE AWARD-WINNING SENSORY PICTURE BOOK

WIGGLES, STOMPS, AND SQUEEZES CALM MY JITTERS DOWN

By

LINDSEY ROWE PARKER

Character Art By

REBECCA BURGESS

Published in the United States by BQB Publishing
(an imprint of Boutique of Quality Books Publishing Company)
www.bqbpublishing.com

978-1-952782-98-5 (p)
978-1-952782-99-2 (e)

Character Art: Rebecca Burgess
Cover and Interior Design: Lindsey Rowe Parker
Interior Design Setup: Robin Krauss, www.bookformatters.com
Editor: Andrea Vande Vorde

HELLO THERE!

Have you ever felt the need for a wiggle, stomp, or squeeze?
You have? Awesome! Me too! Lots of kids do!

Join us in exploring more about why we wiggle, what those jittery feelings are, and how we handle them in different ways!

This fun sensory activity guide is jam-packed with activities that involve your 8 senses. (Yes 8!) Play Sensory Simon Says, decode word scrambles, navigate an obstacle course, reflect on creative prompts, play games, make icky sticky slime, and much more!

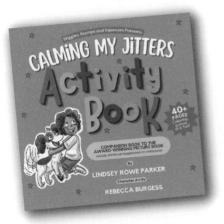

THE WORLD IS BETTER BECAUSE YOU ARE IN IT!

Activities that explore sensory differences help kids to find the language they need to express how they're feeling and better understand themselves. Adding stories and activities about sensory differences to your inclusive library, school, or bookshelf at home empowers kids to feel seen, known, and loved — just as they are.

NOW FOR THE LEGAL STUFF...

Reading through this guide is not a replacement for professional advice or assessment. This guide is intended to introduce the concept of sensory needs, spark conversation with children about sensory differences, foster empathy for these feelings, and identify fun activities that provide sensory input.

PHEW! NOW LET'S HAVE SOME FUN!

LET'S LEARN ABOUT

your 8 Senses

PSSST. YOU'LL SEE A FEW OF THESE QR CODES THROUGHOUT THE BOOK. SCAN THEM TO FIND VIDEOS, BOOK LISTS, AND ACTIVITIES!

SCAN ME

WAIT, THERE ARE 8 SENSES?

Yes, there are 8 senses! We are constantly taking in sensory information from our bodies and environment.

You probably already know the first 5 senses!

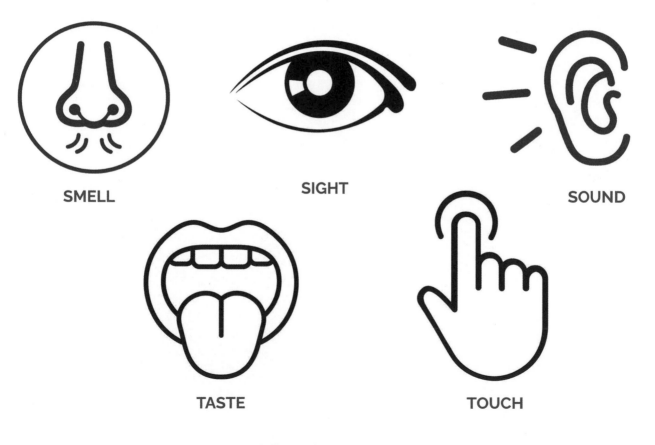

SMELL

SIGHT

SOUND

TASTE

TOUCH

But wait! There are 3 more.
They are:

PROPRIOCEPTION **VESTIBULAR** **INTEROCEPTION**

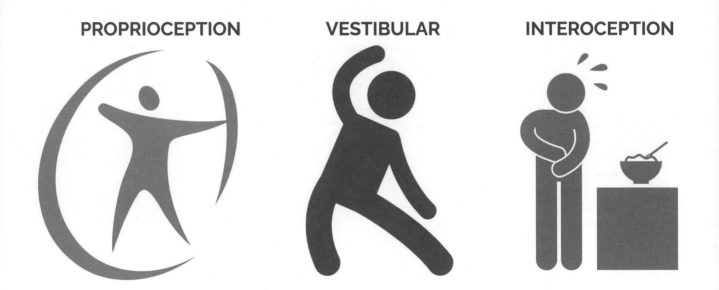

WHOA,
THOSE ARE BIG WORDS.

They are, but you already know the feelings! You feel them every day! Here is an easy glossary for you to understand these new words. **You got this!**

Glossary

PROPRIOCEPTION

This is the hardest one to say. It's a tongue twister! This sense helps us know where your body is in space. That sounds funny, but it is super important. Have you ever bumped into something while walking? Tried to hold an egg in your hand gently without cracking it? This sense helps you feel where you are in relation to things and people.

VESTIBULAR

This sense helps us remain balanced, feel safe when moving, coordinate eye and head movements, and catches us if we start to trip! Try spinning in a circle! Now balance on one foot, then the next!

INTEROCEPTION

This is the sense of knowing what's going on INSIDE our bodies. It's our sense of our internal organs that tells us when we're hungry or full, thirsty, sick, or even need to go to the bathroom. Sometimes we have to pay extra attention to know which feeling is which!

ACTIVITY

Can you identify all 8 senses? Can you think of a time in your day when you use these 3 new senses you just learned? Write or draw them below.

PROPRIOCEPTION — YOUR BODY IN SPACE

VESTIBULAR — BALANCE & MOVEMENT

INTEROCEPTION — INSIDE YOUR BODY

MATCHING

Draw a line to the picture that matches the name of its sense.

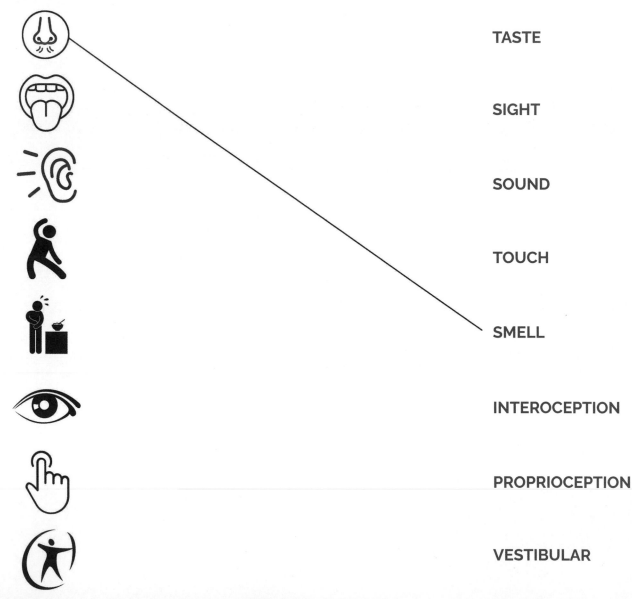

TASTE

SIGHT

SOUND

TOUCH

SMELL

INTEROCEPTION

PROPRIOCEPTION

VESTIBULAR

SENSORY & MOVEMENT ACTIVITIES

 Try different animal walks: Bear walks, crab walks, snake crawls (on belly), frog jumps.

 Push the doorway: Stand in the doorway, reach out your arms, and push against the sides of it as hard as you can. See how many seconds you can push.

 March or jog in place while stomp, stomp, stomping.

 Pour items such as sand, dry beans, dry rice, or water back and forth between containers.

 Squeeze, squish, and smash playdough or slime.

 Try chewy or crunchy foods at snack or mealtime: Celery, carrots, apples, fruit leather, jerky, pita chips.

 Complete an obstacle course or relay race.

LET'S GET MOVING!

SENSORY SIMON SAYS

Stomp in Place	Give yourself a Sqeeze Hug	Crab Walk
Clap your hands	Wiggle	Stretch to the sky
Dance	Plank	Zoom

COLOR THAT SHAPE

What's in this bowl of mush? It smells weird and looks squishy! Follow the color guide and color the shapes. Then count how many of each shape are in the mush and write the number in the boxes below.

ZOOM MAZE

Let's zoom through the house, touching every wall! But wait!
How do we find our way to Mom?

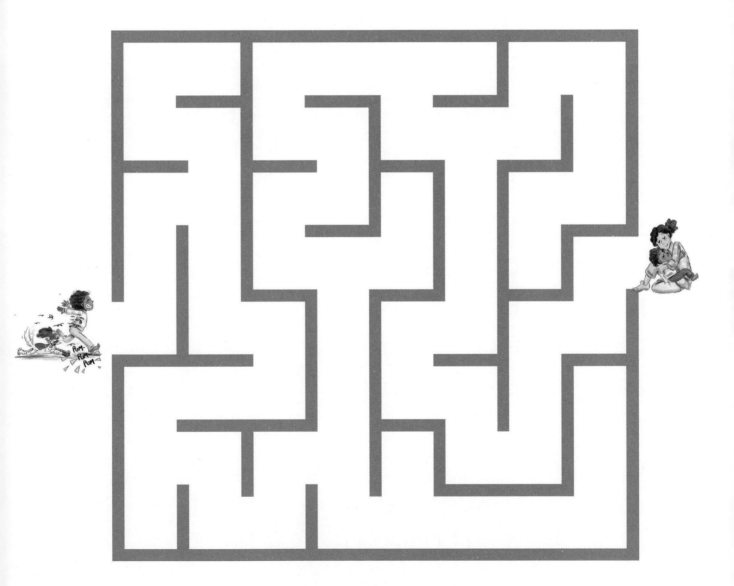

WORD SEARCH

```
T H S Q U I S H Y B Z S D M U
A E M O V E M E N T O B C G S
S E M P A T H Y S M O H R K T
T C G S Q U E E Z E M G M D C
E B D E U U W Q K R P V X M I
A R W I G G L E K Z U I H V S
U E W N P I C T U R E B O O K
S M E L L S T O M P Y B J V M
M D I F F E R E N C E S I E D
C Z W P D C U V D I S O U N D
H F S E N S O R Y C T O U C H
M V I E X T I S I G H T H Q B
Q U A T G P Z V Q V D N E R L
C P J M W A W A R E N E S S S
W K F A J D H U T K V P N K U
```

THESE SNEAKY WORDS ARE HIDING!

picture book	touch
differences	zoom
empathy	sound
awareness	smell
wiggle	movement
stomp	sensory
taste	squeeze
sight	squishy

☑ CALMING ROUTINE

Breathe in ... and out ... Now let's try some calming activities.
How do these make you feel? Which one is your favorite?

☐ Do some stretching

☐ Listen to music you like

☐ Read a favorite story

☐ Do a puzzle

☐ Give someone a big hug

☐ Talk to someone you trust

☐ Play with a calming toy

☐ Go for a walk

☐ Dance around

Rainbow Breathing

Place your finger on the star. Trace each color of the rainbow with your finger as you breathe in and out.

Sensory Play Planner

Monday

_____
_____
_____
_____
_____
_____
_____
_____

Tuesday

_____
_____
_____
_____
_____
_____
_____
_____

Wednesday

_____
_____
_____
_____
_____
_____
_____
_____

Thursday

_____
_____
_____
_____
_____
_____
_____
_____

Friday

_____
_____
_____
_____
_____
_____
_____
_____

Sample

Sensory Simon Says
Blowing Bubbles
Crunchy Snack
Playdough or Slime
Bouncy Action Song
March Around the Room
Obstacle Course
Jump Rope
Read in a Pillow Corner

ICKY STICKY SLIME

Ewwww. Slime can be icky, gooey, sticky, and gross! It can also be oh-so FUN. Here's a super-easy slime recipe to try.

Ingredients

- 8-ounce bottle of Elmer's white school glue
- 1 1/2-2 Tablespoons contact saline solution
- 1 Tablespoon baking soda
- Food coloring, optional

Directions

- Add glue and food coloring to the bowl. Stir until combined.
- Mix in baking soda.
- Add 1 1/2 Tablespoons saline solution and mix until combined.

If it's too sticky, add 1/2 Tablespoon more solution at a time. The more you add, the thicker it'll be. The less you add, the slimier it'll be.

Marvel at your icky sticky masterpiece!

OBSTACLE COURSE

Join Pediatric Occupational Therapist Caitlyn Berry as she shows you how to create a sensory obstacle course with things you probably already have at home!

INDOOR SNOWBALL TOSS

No snow? No problem! We'll play inside! Simply roll up socks into balls. You can use all those socks that don't have a matching one!

Directions

Grab a bucket or container and place it on one side of the room.

Roll your socks into balls. 5-8 is a good number.

Toss the snowballs into the bucket or container.

Use masking tape or painter's tape to mark off a line on the floor a few feet away from the bucket or container. Can you make the shot from all the way across the room?

You can also incorporate this into the obstacle course!

HOW DO YOU FEEL?

Feelings can be complicated. Sometimes it's hard to say how we are feeling. We can always start by identifying if we feel good or bad.

FEELING GOOD?

FEELING BAD?

When you feel good, you might also say you feel...

When you feel bad, you might also say you feel...

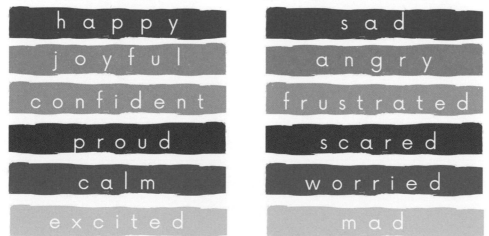

happy	sad
joyful	angry
confident	frustrated
proud	scared
calm	worried
excited	mad

It's okay to feel our feelings!

WRITE OR DRAW WHAT IT FEELS LIKE
TO FEEL STUCK.

WRITE OR DRAW WHAT IT FEELS LIKE

TO EAT SOMETHING WEIRD.

WRITE OR DRAW WHAT IT FEELS LIKE

TO TRY SOMETHING NEW.

WRITE OR DRAW WHAT IT FEELS LIKE

TO FEEL FRUSTRATED.

WRITE OR DRAW WHAT IT FEELS LIKE
TO FEEL JITTERS.

WRITE OR DRAW WHAT IT FEELS LIKE

TO FEEL LOVED.

WRITE OR DRAW WHAT IT FEELS LIKE

TO BE ACCEPTED FOR WHO YOU ARE.

LET'S TALK ABOUT IT!

- What kinds of things are stinky?

- Squishy?

- Crunchy?

- How do you feel when you are on a swing?

- How does wind feel on your face?

- What do you call that feeling when you are running so fast and you feel your feet vibrating on the ground?

40

FRAME IT!

Scan the QR code below to print both the black and white or the color version for your room or classroom! Because it's true, **the world is better because YOU are in it!**

Reading Guide

COMPANION LESSONS FOR THE AWARD-WINNING PICTURE BOOK

WIGGLES, STOMPS, AND SQUEEZES CALM MY JITTERS DOWN

"Wiggles" Stomps and Squeezes Calm My Jitters Down

LINDSEY ROWE PARKER

Illustrated by
REBECCA BURGESS

LET'S ASK QUESTIONS TO FIND ANSWERS!

BEFORE READING

- Identify the parts of the book: cover, title page, illustrations, spine.

- Based on the cover and title of the book, what do you think the story is about?

- Read the summary on the back cover of the book. Now, what do you think the story is about?

- What do you think "jitters" means?

NOW READ THE BOOK, BUT STOP BEFORE THE HANDWASHING SCENE.

- What is the child upset about?

- What is one way you can calm your "jitters" down?

- How do you think this story ends?

- Write your own ending to the story. Draw a picture to go with it.

AFTER READING

- Summarize the story.

- What sounds were repeated in the book?

- Do "jitters" mean something different to you now that you have read the story?

- Why do you think she did not want a hug from her mom at first?

- What changed her mind?

AFTER READING

- Why do you think the water helped her?

- Can you share a time that you felt the "jitters"? What did that feel like?

- Draw your favorite activities to do that make you feel happy and loved.

LOOK THROUGH THE PAGES AGAIN. FOCUS ON THE ILLUSTRATIONS.

- Do you recognize the five senses in this book? Are there more?

- Do you know we have eight senses? What are they?

- Where do you see those senses in the story?

- Do you see the dog in the book? What are they doing?

- Who is sitting at the table? What are they doing?

MEET THE CREATORS

Lindsey Rowe Parker: Author

Lindsey Rowe Parker is a neurodivergent author and mom of multiple sensory kids! With an adult diagnosis of ADHD and a new deeper understanding of her own sensory experiences, she has begun to delve into the neurodiversity community, learning all she can from neurodivergent voices.

She is author of the award-winning book about sensory differences, **Wiggles, Stomps, and Squeezes Calm My Jitters Down**, and she hopes it connects with everyone who has felt the need for a wiggle, stomp, or squeeze!

Rebecca Burgess: Illustrator

Rebecca is an autistic illustrator living in the UK. They love history and nature, but comics and illustration most of all! Their passion has led them to work with the likes of **The Guardian** and Jessica Kingsley Publishing. Rebecca is most famous for their online comic **"Understanding the Spectrum,"** a comic explaining autism that has been shared in several books and used by parents, teachers, and doctors. Being autistic, they are particularly passionate about bringing more autistic characters into comics and stories!

WE ARE SO GLAD YOU FOUND US!

Visit our website

wigglesstompsandsqueezes.com

Wiggles, Stomps & Squeezes Calm My Jitters Down

Virtual Author Read-Alongs in English, Spanish, and ASL

Follow us on Social Media!

wigglesstompsandsque...

363 Posts 8,533 Followers 4,329 Following

Wiggles, Stomps and Squeezes
A picture book about sensory differences. 📖 in English & Spanish 🎉 | By @lindseyroweparker Illustrated by @theorahart | Celebrating #neurodiversity
linktr.ee/wigglesbook
Followed by make_momentos, youdontneedanagency_ and 62 others

Following ∨   Message

#SensoryStori... Autism Positi... Press Reviews You

LIBRARY REQUEST FORM
Wiggles, Stomps, and Squeezes Calm My Jitters Down

REASON FOR REQUEST:

Please consider purchasing the following picture book titles to add to the library! Sensory differences affect many children and adults, especially those who are neurodivergent, ADHD, or autistic. This book follows a young girl with heightened sensory experiences throughout her day, and how she is able to calm her jitters down with everyday sensory input. This book is available in both English and Spanish.

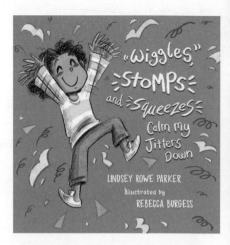

Wiggles, Stomps, and Squeezes Calm My Jitters Down

The vibration in her feet when she runs, the tap-tap-tap of her fork on the table at mealtime, the trickle of cool water running over her hands — these are the things that calm her jitters down.

This book is for anyone who has ever felt the need for a wiggle stomp, or squeeze!

ISBN-10: 194544892X
ISBN-13: 978-1945448928

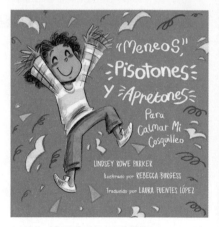

Meneos, Pisotones, Y Apretones Para Calmar Mi Cosquilleo

Ésta es una historia sobre las necesidades sensoriales y de cómo algunos niños y niñas experimentan su mundo, contada desde la perspectiva de una niña.

La vibración en sus pies cuando corre, el tan-tan-tan de su cuchara en la mesa a la hora de comer, el chorrito de agua fría corriendo por sus manos — esas son las cosas que calman su cosquilleo.

¡Este libro es para cualquier persona que alguna vez haya sentido la necesidad de moverse pisotear, o recibir un apretón!

ISBN-10 : 1952782252
ISBN-13 : 978-1952782251

Title Information:

Publisher: BQB Publishing (April 1, 2021)
Author: Lindsey Rowe Parker
Illustrator: Rebecca Burgess
Translator: Laura Fuenetes López
Language: English & Spanish available
Hardcover: 50 pages
Reading age: 5-7 years
Grade level: Kindergarten-Grade 2